Ignorance is BLISS

By Heather Down

Cover Illustration by Design Dynamics
Typography by MarketForce

Published by Great Quotations Publishing Co.,
Glendale Heights, IL

Library of Congress Catalog Card Number: 97-77639

ISBN 1-56245-332-7

Printed in U.S.A

INTRODUCTION

There are many universal questions of the world that philosophers, religious leaders, scientists and mystics have tried to answer, *"Where did we come from? Where are we going? What is the meaning of life?"* For men it has always been questions like, *"Where does folded laundry come from?"*

True, like the early misguided philosophers who thought the world was flat, some of the male species think they have the answers, yet many continue to revel happily in the darkness of half truths. Often, this ignorance can leave the female species feeling unappreciated, undervalued and taken for granted.

I am here to dispel myths, open eyes and share the real meaning of life. My purpose is to be bold enough to ask those earth shattering questions, share the common misconceptions and set the world a spin. After all, the world *is* round!

Where do babies come from?

HE THINKS:

"A ten minute romp in the back seat of a chevy."

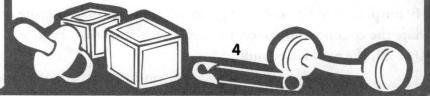

4

SHE KNOWS:

"Nine months of painstaking morning sickness, water retention and varicose veins highlighted by 36 hours of excruciating "touch me and I'll kill you" labor, ending in an epidural and stitches."

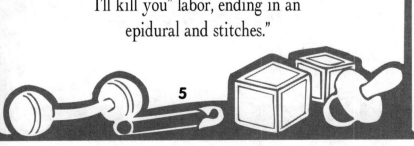

5

How does the toilet get cleaned?

HE THINKS:

"A little blue duck does it."

6

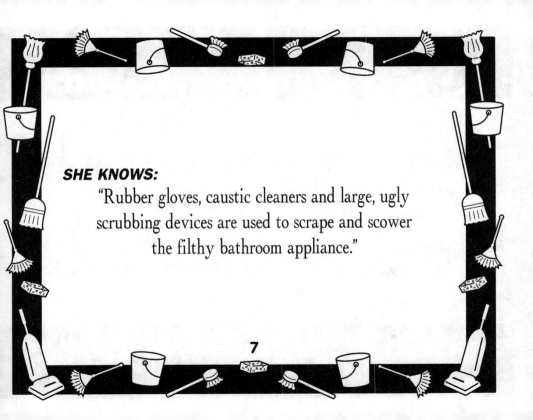

SHE KNOWS:
"Rubber gloves, caustic cleaners and large, ugly scrubbing devices are used to scrape and scower the filthy bathroom appliance."

7

Where does new underwear come from?

HE THINKS:

"It grows on a fruit of the loom tree."

SHE KNOWS:

"When the elastic waist band becomes less elastic and actually a bigger
circumference than the fabric, the perfect brand, size and color
is carefully selected from a quality department store, washed,
then placed in the appropriate drawer."

Where does a clean spoon come from?

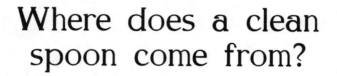

HE THINKS:

"A kitchen drawer."

10

SHE KNOWS:

"The spoon is collected from the sticky ice cream bowl that was left by the TV three weeks ago. Soap is put in a kitchen basin called a sink and it is then filled with very hot water where the spoon is scrubbed with a clean cloth, dried and put away."

11

Why don't shirts have wrinkles?

HE THINKS:

"You mean cotton wrinkles?"

12

SHE KNOWS:

"Wrinkle-less shirts are ones that have been boldly washed, dried, shaken and pressed into submission after using up a can of starch and the hottest iron on the market to fight those pesky, ever-present wrinkles."

13

Where do anniversary presents come from?

HE THINKS:

"The drug store."

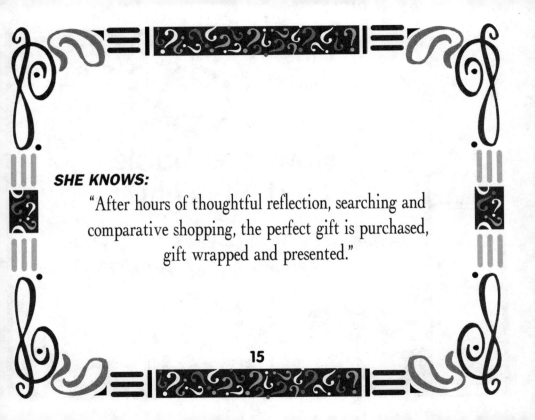

SHE KNOWS:

"After hours of thoughtful reflection, searching and comparative shopping, the perfect gift is purchased, gift wrapped and presented."

How are babies fed at night?

HE THINKS:

"Babies eat at night?"

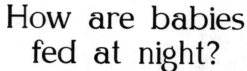

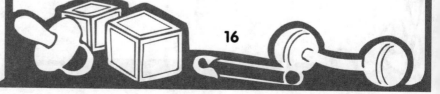

16

SHE KNOWS:

"A loving care-giver groggily gets out of bed to calm
the screaming infant. The baby is given sustenance,
rocked and walked until it finally falls back
to sleep – usually as the sun begins to rise."

17

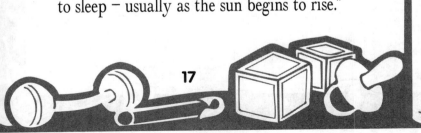

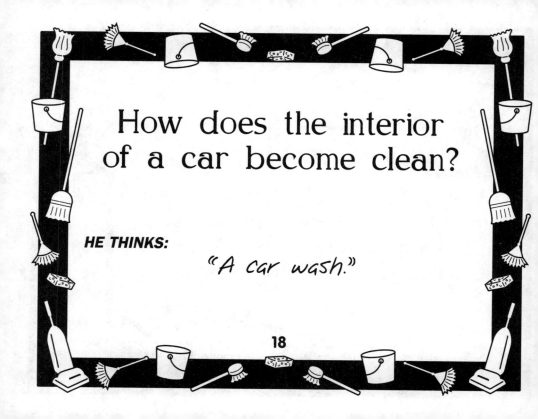

How does the interior
of a car become clean?

HE THINKS:

"A car wash."

18

SHE KNOWS:

"After removing the kids, transporting a multitude of grocery bags from the trunk and back seat and removing the gummy bears from countless crevices in the cushions, a vacuum cleaner, solvents and disinfectants are used for three hours to clean the car."

How do children become talented?

HE THINKS:

"It's in the genes."

SHE KNOWS:

> "Endless days of playing chauffeur to hockey practices, piano lessons, dance classes, parent/teacher interviews, scout meetings and track club."

Where does Christmas dinner come from?

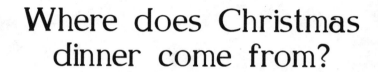

HE THINKS:

"The oven."

22

SHE KNOWS:

"A turkey is specially selected several days in advance. It is stuffed, cooked and served with care with great-grandmother's secret stuffing recipe that takes two days to make properly. Vegetables, salads and potatoes are all carefully prepared with precision timing so that everything can be served piping-hot at the same time."

23

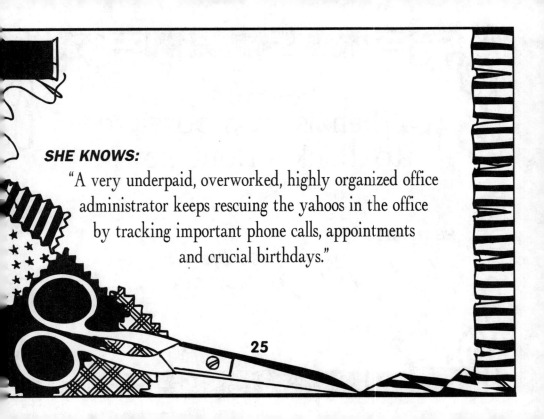

SHE KNOWS:

"A very underpaid, overworked, highly organized office administrator keeps rescuing the yahoos in the office by tracking important phone calls, appointments and crucial birthdays."

25

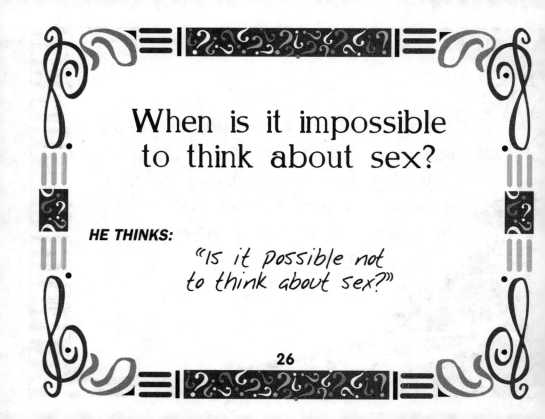

When is it impossible to think about sex?

HE THINKS:

"Is it possible not to think about sex?"

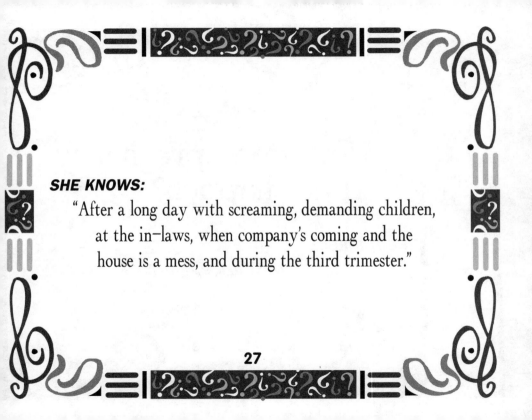

SHE KNOWS:

"After a long day with screaming, demanding children, at the in-laws, when company's coming and the house is a mess, and during the third trimester."

How does pregnancy happen?

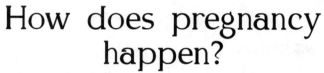

HE THINKS:

"Misconceptions?"

28

SHE KNOWS:

"Conceptions."

29

Where do clean windows come from?

HE THINKS:

"They are installed once a week."

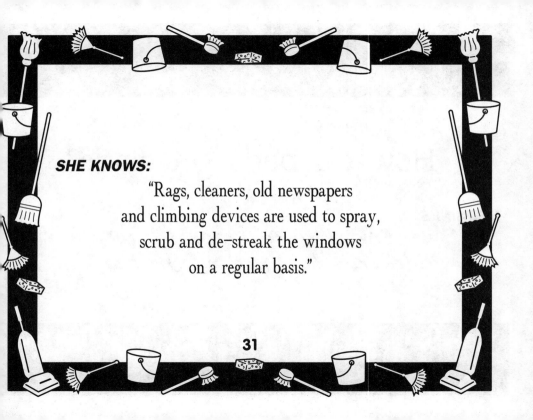

SHE KNOWS:

"Rags, cleaners, old newspapers
and climbing devices are used to spray,
scrub and de-streak the windows
on a regular basis."

31

How do beds get made?

HE THINKS:

"By shoving the covers up towards the head of the bed."

SHE KNOWS:

"Starting with the bottom sheet, each strata of the bed is carefully centered, smoothed and tucked. When the final layer is reached the pillows are neatly placed at the head of the bed."

Where does coffee come from?

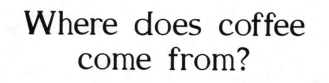

HE THINKS:

"The pot."

34

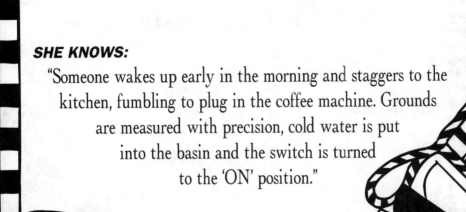

SHE KNOWS:

"Someone wakes up early in the morning and staggers to the kitchen, fumbling to plug in the coffee machine. Grounds are measured with precision, cold water is put into the basin and the switch is turned to the 'ON' position."

35

How are the floors cleaned?

HE THINKS:

"Dirt is brushed under the carpet."

SHE KNOWS:

"A large, heavy device called a vacuum cleaner is used every few days to suck up all the shoe grime, dog hair, food crumbs and 'child goo' that perpetually accumulates on the floor."

37

What goes into planning a wedding?

HE THINKS:

"Finding a stripper for the bachelor party."

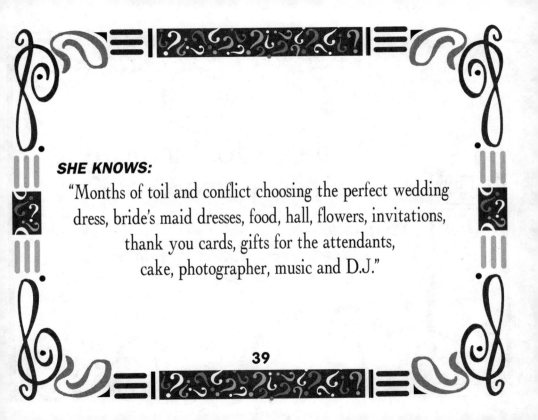

SHE KNOWS:

"Months of toil and conflict choosing the perfect wedding dress, bride's maid dresses, food, hall, flowers, invitations, thank you cards, gifts for the attendants, cake, photographer, music and D.J."

Where do birthday cakes come from?

HE THINKS:

"Does 7-11 have a bakery?"

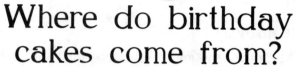

40

SHE KNOWS:

"Birthday cakes are ordered or baked in advance.
The interests, personality and nuances of the
birthday person are considered before flavor,
color and icing are chosen."

41

How does the piano get dusted?

HE THINKS:

"The kids bang on it."

SHE KNOWS:

"The outer wood is polished with a high quality oil. Then, the ivory keys are wiped individually with a damp cloth. The strings and back are vacuumed with a special brush attachment."

Who is the tooth fairy?

HE THINKS:

"The lady who flies around at night gathering children's teeth in exchange for money."

SHE KNOWS:

"A responsible adult who wakes up in the middle of the night to fish out a microscopic tooth from underneath covers, pillows, stuffed animals and a kid in exchange for some hard earned cash in order to perpetuate an urban myth called the tooth fairy."

How do you get stains out of clothes?

HE THINKS:

"Buy new clothes."

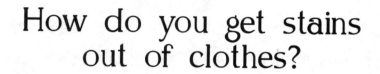

46

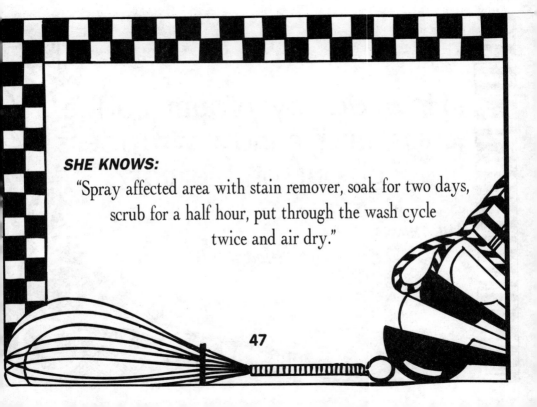

SHE KNOWS:

"Spray affected area with stain remover, soak for two days, scrub for a half hour, put through the wash cycle twice and air dry."

How do styrofoam coffee cups and candy wrappers get out of the car?

HE THINKS:

"The wind blows them out."

48

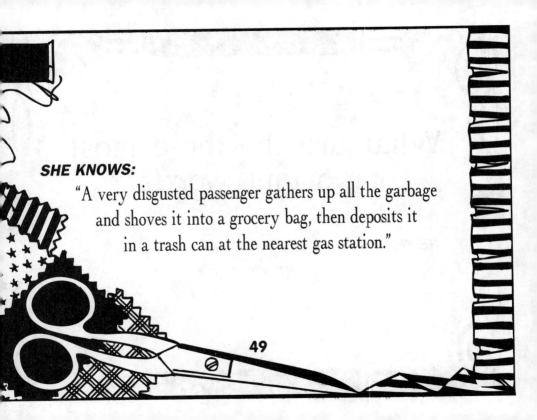

SHE KNOWS:

"A very disgusted passenger gathers up all the garbage and shoves it into a grocery bag, then deposits it in a trash can at the nearest gas station."

49

What are the three most important words?

HE THINKS:

"I am hungry."

SHE KNOWS:

"I love you."

Where do Christmas presents for the kids come from?

HE THINKS:

"Santa Claus."

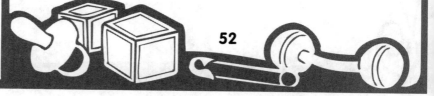

52

SHE KNOWS:

"Someone battles relentless, crowded malls looking
for those dearly requested, over–priced treasures
that can't be found anywhere on the continent.
The presents are hidden, wrapped and put under
the tree on Christmas Eve without detection."

53

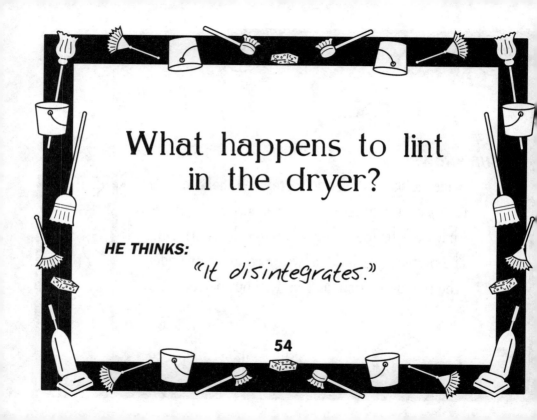

What happens to lint in the dryer?

HE THINKS:

"It disintegrates."

54

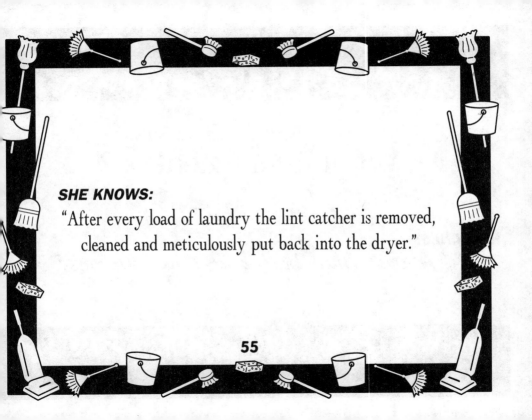

SHE KNOWS:

"After every load of laundry the lint catcher is removed, cleaned and meticulously put back into the dryer."

55

What is a vacation?

HE THINKS:

"*A boat, live bait and some buddies.*"

"Leaving the kids at the in-laws, flying to a very private, warm island, staying in a 5 star hotel and relaxing in the hot tub."

Where do clean sheets come from?

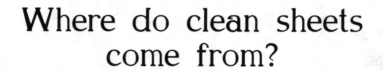

HE THINKS:

"The linen drawer."

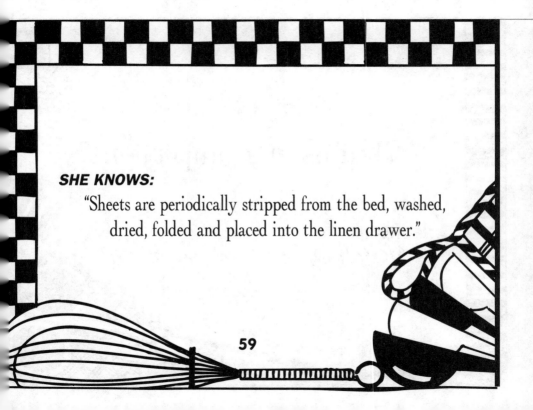

SHE KNOWS:

"Sheets are periodically stripped from the bed, washed,
dried, folded and placed into the linen drawer."

59

What is a compliment?

HE THINKS:
"Ketchup, mustard or relish."

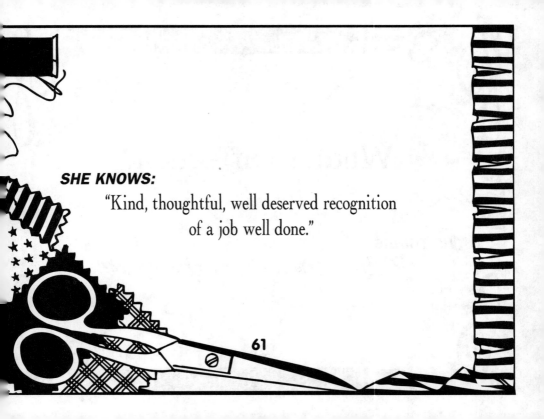

SHE KNOWS:

"Kind, thoughtful, well deserved recognition of a job well done."

61

What is affection?

HE THINKS:

"Patting the dog on the head."

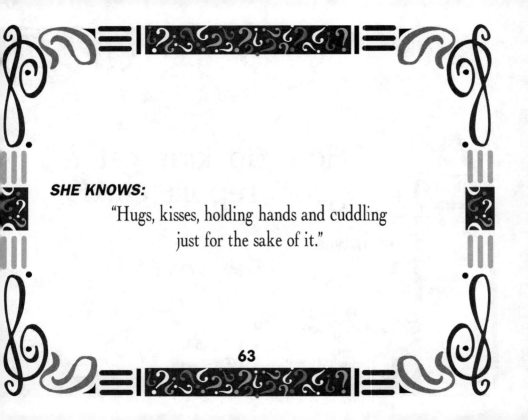

SHE KNOWS:

"Hugs, kisses, holding hands and cuddling
just for the sake of it."

How do kids get a good report card?

HE THINKS:

"They cheat."

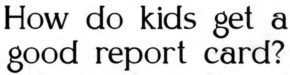

64

SHE KNOWS:

"Someone spends 2 hours each evening helping them to learn the life cycles of moths, the meaning of integers and other important life skills. Entire days are spent volunteering in the classroom and supervising on field trips."

65

Where do outdated clothes go?

HE THINKS:

"What did you do with my blue tux?"

66

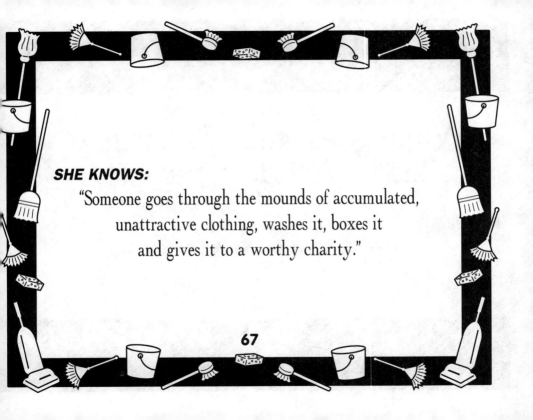

SHE KNOWS:
"Someone goes through the mounds of accumulated, unattractive clothing, washes it, boxes it and gives it to a worthy charity."

67

What goes into planning a kid's birthday party?

HE THINKS:

"A cake and some balloons."

SHE KNOWS:

"Invitations, kid friendly food, party hats, streamers, balloons,
a pre-ordered designer cake, numerous games, a live clown,
pony rides, a good video and lots of patience."

Where does the change on the dresser go?

HE THINKS:

"To her purse."

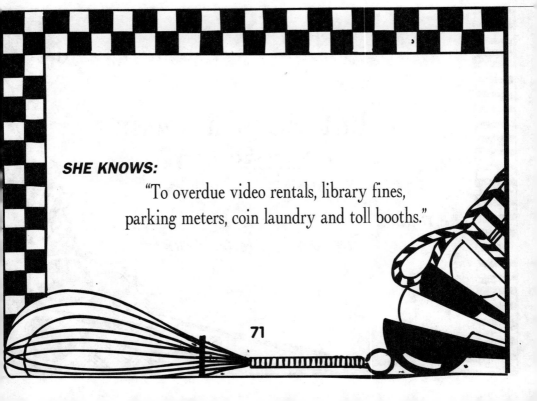

SHE KNOWS:

"To overdue video rentals, library fines, parking meters, coin laundry and toll booths."

71

What does it mean to 'dress up'?

HE THINKS:

"Put on a clean shirt."

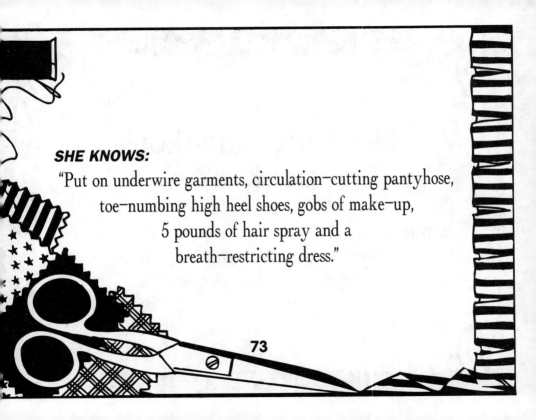

SHE KNOWS:

"Put on underwire garments, circulation-cutting pantyhose,
toe-numbing high heel shoes, gobs of make-up,
5 pounds of hair spray and a
breath-restricting dress."

73

How are vacations booked?

HE THINKS:

"We go to the airport and get on the plane."

SHE KNOWS:

"Ten months in advance all the major airlines are contacted to compare prices, packages and value. Luggage, baby sitters, kennels for the dogs, someone to pick up the mail, traveller checks, tickets and hotel reservations are then put in place and on the day of departure we go to the airport and get on the plane."

How do the pets get fed?

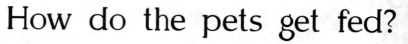

HE THINKS:

"They are hunter-gathers."

76

SHE KNOWS:

"Someone buys food at the pet store, brings it home and stores it in a cool, dry place. The pets are then given kind appropriate rations on a daily basis."

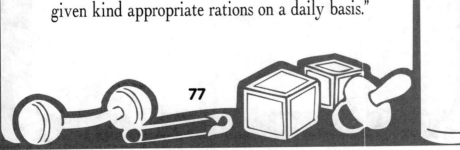

77

How does the toilet seat get put back down?

HE THINKS:

"Gravity."

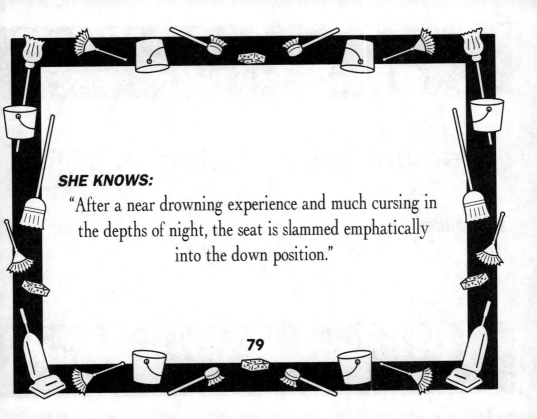

SHE KNOWS:

"After a near drowning experience and much cursing in the depths of night, the seat is slammed emphatically into the down position."

79

How are doors locked at night?

HE THINKS:

"Automatically."

SHE KNOWS:

"Each night the front and back doors are locked and checked by a sleepy but dedicated home owner in an effort to keep out unwanted guests."

How does the lid get back on the toothpaste?

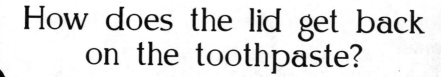

HE THINKS:

"It's never taken off."

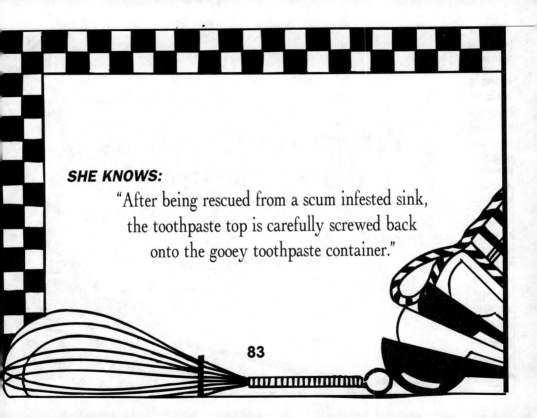

SHE KNOWS:

"After being rescued from a scum infested sink,
the toothpaste top is carefully screwed back
onto the gooey toothpaste container."

83

Where do Christmas cards come from?

HE THINKS:

"The North pole."

84

SHE KNOWS:

"Once a year thoughtful people remember friends, relatives and colleagues by sending them a lovely, selectively chosen, neatly-addressed Christmas card, scented with perfume and topped with appropriate postage."

85

What is the perfect evening at home?

HE THINKS:

"A commercial-free Baywatch-a-thon."

SHE KNOWS:

"A fire in the fireplace, kids tucked into bed,
a good book and classical music."

Where do mother-in-laws come from?

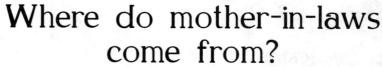

HE THINKS:

"A very deep, dark place."

88

SHE KNOWS:

"They come from a background of very patient nurturing, raising and caring for their precious daughter in hopes that she would accomplish great things....
and marry a millionaire."

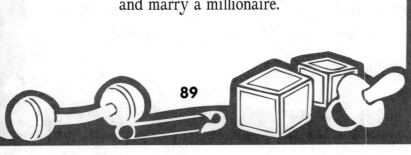

89

Where does folded laundry come from?

HE THINKS:

"It spontaneously regenerates itself on a weekly basis in the drawers and closets of the house."

90

SHE KNOWS:

"After it is collected from the laundry basket, fished out
from under the bed and picked up off the bathroom floor,
it is then sorted and transported to the big white machine
in the basement called a washer where it is washed,
rinsed and put into a dryer, then folded, ironed and
put back in the drawers and closets of origin.

91

How are socks matched?

HE THINKS:

"They go toe-to-toe in the drawer and tango."

"After the dryer has eaten its weekly quota, they are unballed, turned right side out, sorted and carefully rolled."

What does it mean to "eat your greens?"

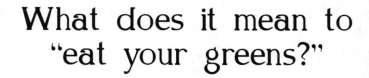

HE THINKS:

"Swallowing the mold on the bottom of a hot dog bun."

94

"After careful consideration of all the essential vitamins necessary for a healthy body, a variety of green, leafy vegetables are scrutinized for selection at the grocery store, then lovingly prepared to help in the prevention of a variety of very scary diseases."

How do strapless dresses stay up?

HE THINKS:

"Duct tape."

96

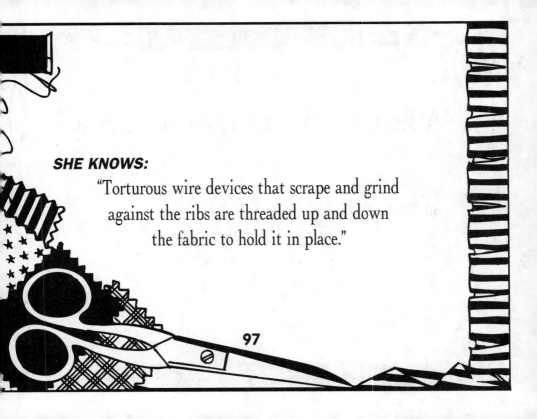

SHE KNOWS:

"Torturous wire devices that scrape and grind
against the ribs are threaded up and down
the fabric to hold it in place."

97

What is a hormonal cycle?

HE THINKS:

"Something bigger than a tricycle."

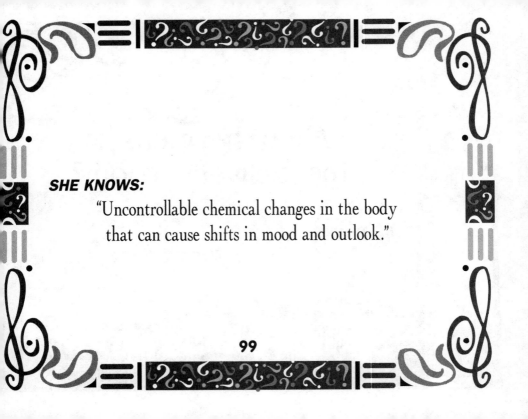

SHE KNOWS:

"Uncontrollable chemical changes in the body that can cause shifts in mood and outlook."

What happens in the delivery room?

HE THINKS:

"Men pass out."

SHE KNOWS:

"A woman screams, pushes, huffs, sweats to the beat of the newborn and wishes she could pass out, making any aerobics class look like a picnic."

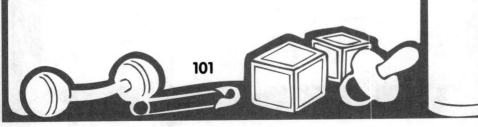

101

How does the fish tank get cleaned?

HE THINKS:

"The filter."

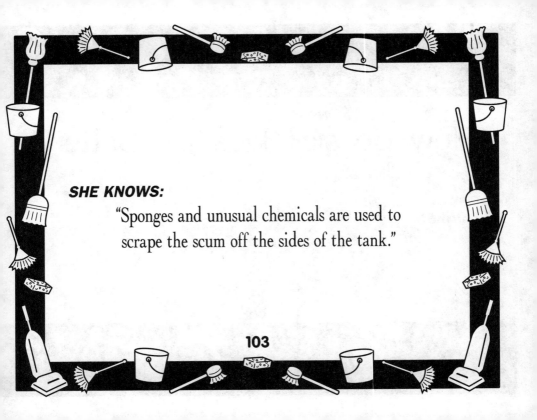

SHE KNOWS:

"Sponges and unusual chemicals are used to scrape the scum off the sides of the tank."

How do sick kids get better?

HE THINKS:

"Time and Tylenol."

SHE KNOWS:

> "After numerous trips to the Doctor's office,
> endless crying through the night, cranky days,
> bottles of 'anything–but–cherry–flavored' medicine
> that often gets spit up and time."

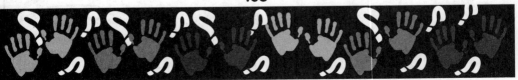

How does the juice container refill itself?

HE THINKS:

"There is a juice dispenser built into the fridge."

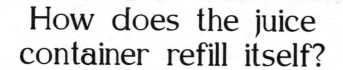

SHE KNOWS:

"Someone rescues the empty jug and gets a can opener which only opens half the lid and the juice lump is prodded out with a fork. Then, 3 cans of water are added and a potato masher is used to squash the rock solid piece of juice in attempts of mixing it."

How does the phone get answered?

HE THINKS:

"It doesn't if I'm doing something important, like watching T.V."

SHE KNOWS:

"A very busy person drops whatever is being done
in order to rush to pick up the receiver,
talk and take messages."

What is needed to make a woman look beautiful?

HE THINKS:

"A hair brush."

SHE KNOWS:

"Facials, exfoliants, mortgage-your-house priced skin care products, contact lenses, blow dryers, hot rollers, daily aerobics classes, liposuction, cosmetic surgery, implants, hair color, hair removal products, kill-your-feet shoes and, of course, a hair brush."

What is PMS?

HE THINKS:

"*Time to go out with the boys!*"

112

SHE KNOWS:

"Bloating, water retention, cramps, mood changes and uncontrollable hormonal swings that attack the body on a monthly basis."

113

How does a wet bath mat get hung up?

HE THINKS:

"You can hang those things up?"

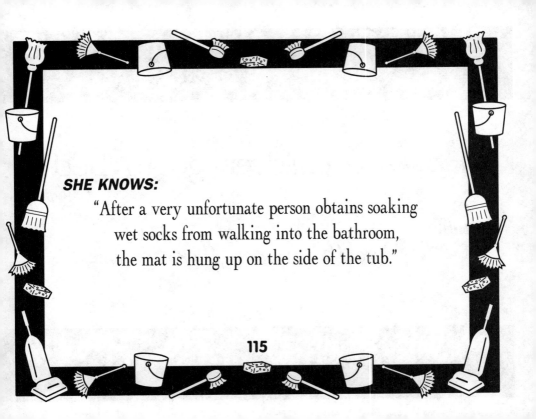

SHE KNOWS:

"After a very unfortunate person obtains soaking wet socks from walking into the bathroom, the mat is hung up on the side of the tub."

How do children go to bed?

HE THINKS:

"They go there when they are tired."

SHE KNOWS:

> "After bathing them against their will, forcing them to change into pajamas, coaxing them to brush their teeth, reading them several stories, singing to them and rocking them, they drift peacefully into sleep."

What is the most useful household appliance?

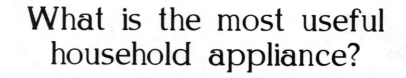

HE THINKS:

"The remote control."

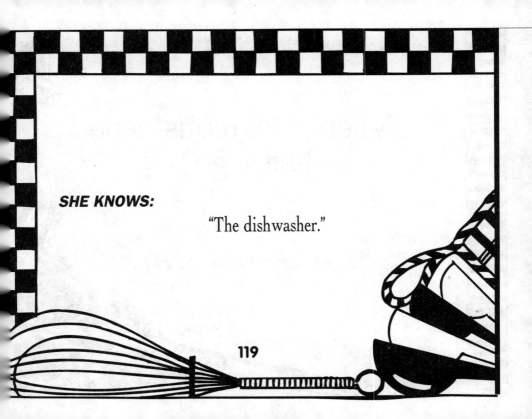

SHE KNOWS:

"The dishwasher."

119

SHE KNOWS:

"After they are shaved off they are gathered up off the counter, sink and floor to be thrown out, flushed or washed down the drain."

121

What is needed for a romantic evening?

HE THINKS:

"Clean shorts and a trip to the adult video store."

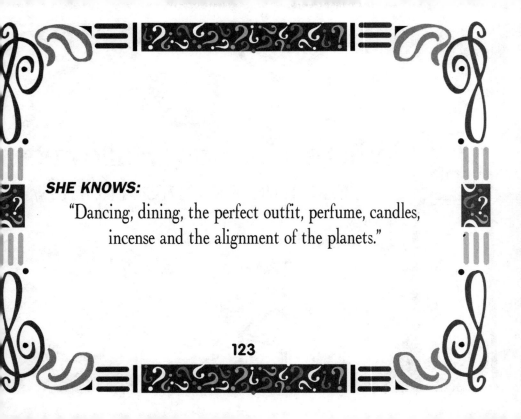

SHE KNOWS:

"Dancing, dining, the perfect outfit, perfume, candles, incense and the alignment of the planets."

Where do kids' Halloween costumes come from?

HE THINKS:

"The thrift shop?"

124

SHE KNOWS:

"After much thought and consideration a costume idea is conceived. Then, after many visits to the craft, fabric and department stores, the masterpiece is skillfully put together to create an exciting facade for the ghoulish evening."

125

Where do the globs of toothpaste in the sink go?

HE THINKS:

"Isn't that where they are suppose to be?"

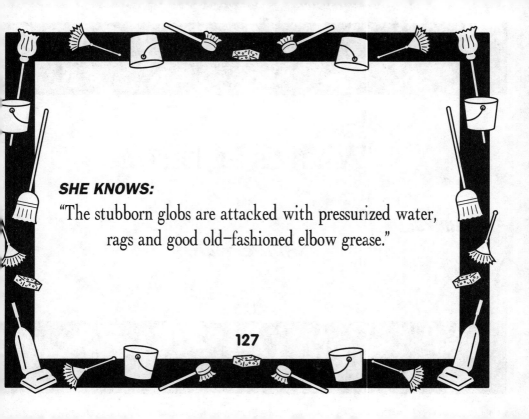

SHE KNOWS:
"The stubborn globs are attacked with pressurized water, rags and good old-fashioned elbow grease."

127

What is a hero?

HE THINKS:

"Spiderman."

SHE KNOWS:

"Anyone who offers to take the kids for an afternoon."

How does a table get set?

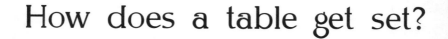

HE THINKS:

"A plate, fork and cup are thrown down at each place."

130

SHE KNOWS:

"Table cloths, plates, salad forks, main course forks, dessert forks, knives, spoons, cups, napkins and dessert plates are placed in the appropriate spot at each setting."

131

How do pants get hemmed?

HE THINKS:

"A stapler at the office."

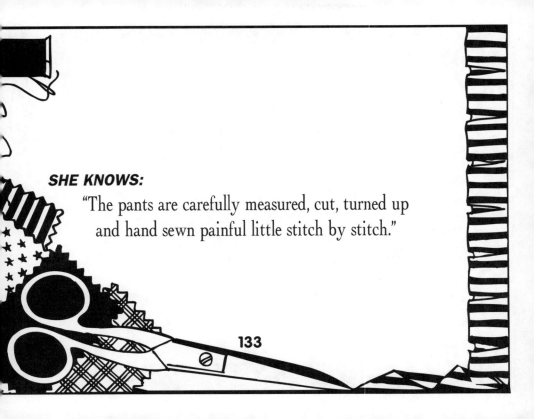

SHE KNOWS:

"The pants are carefully measured, cut, turned up and hand sewn painful little stitch by stitch."

133

What is a budget?

HE THINKS:

"Something your parents used."

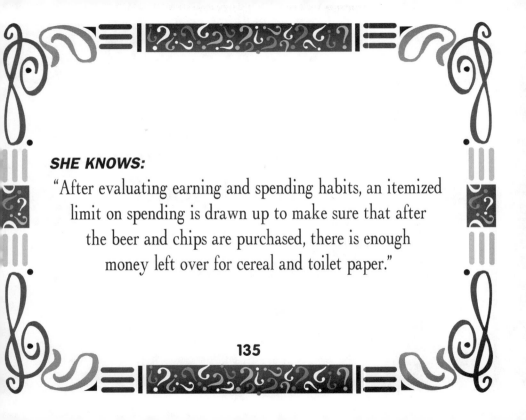

SHE KNOWS:

"After evaluating earning and spending habits, an itemized
limit on spending is drawn up to make sure that after
the beer and chips are purchased, there is enough
money left over for cereal and toilet paper."

Why do babies smell good?

HE THINKS:

"They are still new."

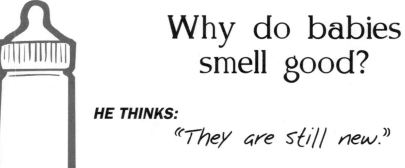

136

SHE KNOWS:

"Their messy, dirty diapers are changed regularly,
then various powders and creams are applied to
give off a sweet, potpourri scent."

137

Where do wet towels go?

HE THINKS:

"They are bunched up in a ball and thrown on the floor."

138

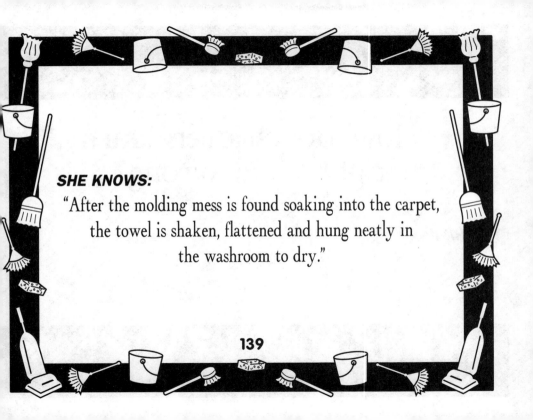

SHE KNOWS:

"After the molding mess is found soaking into the carpet, the towel is shaken, flattened and hung neatly in the washroom to dry."

139

How do children learn right from wrong?

HE THINKS:

"Watching T.V."

"Careful guidance, appropriate consequences, time–outs,
caring instruction, a living example and loving communication."

What goes into a gourmet dinner?

HE THINKS:

"The colonel's best and a bottle of root beer."

142

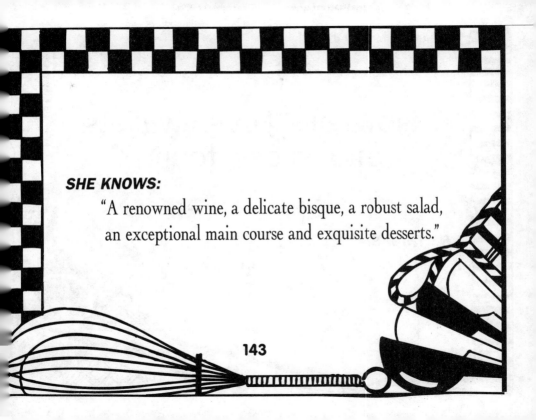

SHE KNOWS:

"A renowned wine, a delicate bisque, a robust salad, an exceptional main course and exquisite desserts."

143

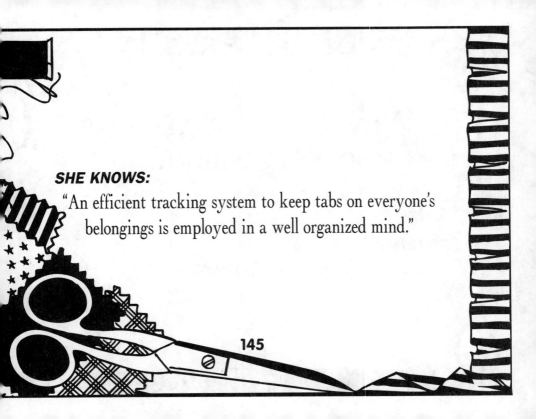

SHE KNOWS:

"An efficient tracking system to keep tabs on everyone's belongings is employed in a well organized mind."

145

Why are women's legs so silky smooth?

HE THINKS:

"The X-chromosome."

SHE KNOWS:

"Root-ripping waxes, razors that cut and scrape, shock therapy and smelly depilatories."

What is menopause?

HE THINKS:

"When I stop and think for a minute."

148

SHE KNOWS:

"Hormonal swings, hot flashes, estrogen pills and uneasiness that seems to last for eons."

149

How does the alarm get set?

HE THINKS:

"Alarms are set?"

SHE KNOWS:

"Faithfully, the alarm is set, checked,
then re-checked to see that it will go off
in time to keep people from being fired."

How do library books get returned?

HE THINKS:

"They're supposed to be returned?"

SHE KNOWS:

"A conscientious person finds the over-due books stuffed between the mattresses, in the cushions of the couch or in the back seat of the car. They are then driven to the library and returned so all fines can be paid."

What is intuition?

HE THINKS:

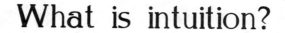

"Something I don't have."

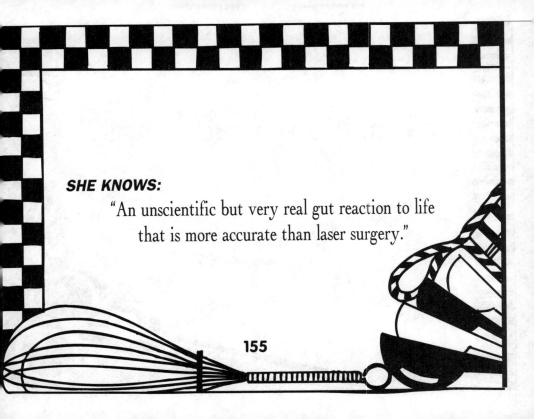

SHE KNOWS:

"An unscientific but very real gut reaction to life that is more accurate than laser surgery."

What are road maps?

HE THINKS:

"An unmanly sign of weakness."

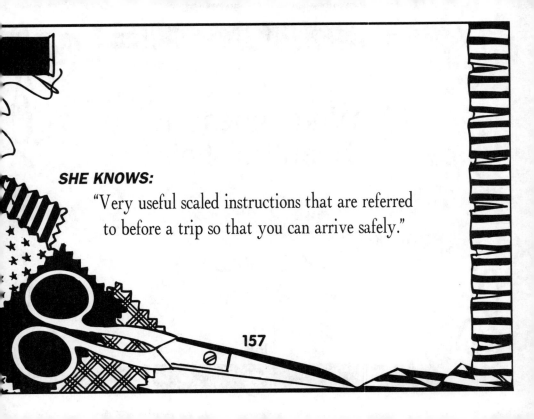

SHE KNOWS:

"Very useful scaled instructions that are referred to before a trip so that you can arrive safely."

157

What goes into beautiful hair?

HE THINKS:

"Shampoo."

SHE KNOWS:

"An excellent hairdresser, monthly trims,
to-die-for-hair color, high lights, boar-bristled brushes,
blow dryers, mousse, gel, spray, curling irons, hot roller
and quality shampoos and conditioners."

What is the perfect anniversary gift?

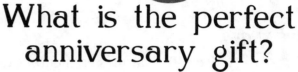

HE THINKS:

"A bowling ball with your husband's name on it."

160

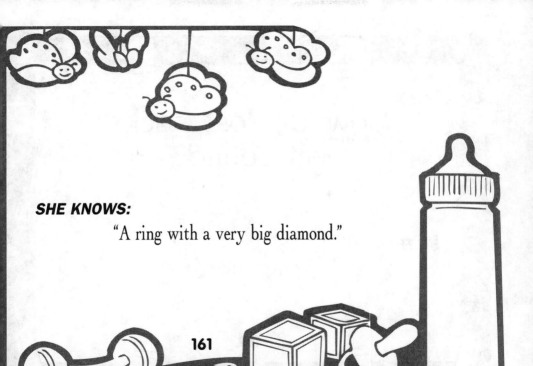

SHE KNOWS:

"A ring with a very big diamond."

161

How do lost socks get found?

HE THINKS:

"They don't."

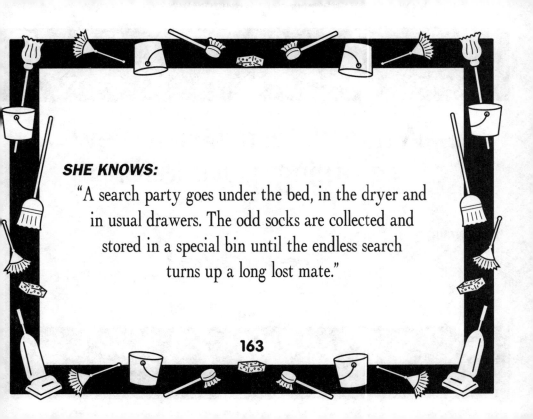

SHE KNOWS:

"A search party goes under the bed, in the dryer and in usual drawers. The odd socks are collected and stored in a special bin until the endless search turns up a long lost mate."

163

What determines a new clothing purchase?

HE THINKS:

"The price tag."

SHE KNOWS:

"The brand, quality, color, texture, style, threading and the price of the garment compared to the 500 others tried on that day."

What is a karat?

HE THINKS:

"An orange vegetable my
mother made me eat."

SHE KNOWS:

"A way of measuring the worth of gold or diamonds when either is found in engagement, wedding, anniversary and 'just because' rings."

167

Other Titles by Great Quotations

GREAT QUOTATIONS PUBLISHING COMPANY

Glendale Heights, IL 60139

Phone (630) 582-2800 • Fax (630) 582-2813

168